A Pumpkin Full of Poems

Illustrated by Sheilah Beckett

Happy House Books

Copyright © 1982 by Random House, Inc. All rights reserved under International and Pan-American Copyright Conventions. Published in the United States by Random House, Inc., New York, and simultaneously in Canada by Random House of Canada Limited, Toronto. ISBN: 0-394-85000-9 Library of Congress Catalog Card Number: 81-52178
Manufactured in the United States of America   1 2 3 4 5 6 7 8 9 0

On Halloween

The witches fly
Across the sky.
The owls go "Who? Who? Who?"
The black cats yowl
And the green ghosts howl,
"Scary Halloween to you!"

Nina Willis Walter

Pumpkin

We bought a fat
    orange pumpkin,
The plumpest sort
    they sell.

We neatly scooped
    the inside out
And only left
    the shell.

We carved a funny
   funny-face
Of silly shape
   and size,
A pointy nose,
   a jagged mouth
And two enormous eyes.

We set it in a window
And we put
   a candle in,
Then lit it up
   for all to see
Our jack-o'-lantern grin.

Jack Prelutsky

Hallowe'en

Tonight is the night
When leaves make a sound
Like a gnome in his home
Under the ground,
When spooks and trolls
Creep out of holes
Mossy and green.

Tonight is the night
When pumpkins stare
Through sheaves and leaves
Everywhere,
When ghoul and ghost
And goblin host
Dance round their queen.
It's Hallowe'en.

Harry Behn

Creepy

When I go out to trick or treat,
I feel a little fright.
There's lots of goblins on the loose,
And monsters out at night.

Who knows what lurks behind that door,
Or hides around that tree?
So just to play it extra safe,
I take my Dad with me!

Keith Hall, Jr.

What Should I Be for Halloween?

It's Halloween! What should I be?
A devil? A tulip? A bumblebee?
A beggar? A robber? Or maybe a wizard?
A princess, a lion, a mouse or a lizard?
I could be a cockroach, I could be a goose,
I could be a kitten, or even a moose,
I could be a ghost, or a movie star,
I could even dress up as a candy bar!
Most nights, of course, I can't choose who to be—
and most of the time, I enjoy being me—
but tonight I'll dress up and get good things to eat,
'Cause it's Halloween night . . . TRICK OR TREAT!

Deborah Hautzig

Fall

The last of October
We lock the garden gate.
(The flowers have all withered
That used to stand straight.)

The last of October
We put the swings away
And the porch looks deserted
Where we liked to play.

The last of October
The birds have all flown,
The screens are in the attic,
The sandpile's alone.

Everything is put away
Before it starts to snow—
I wonder if the ladybugs
Have any place to go!

Aileen Fisher

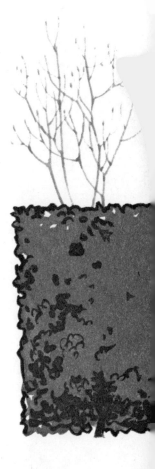

Hallowe'en

The moon is round as a jack-o'-lantern;
The trees blow black and bare;
And we go creeping with spooky giggles
Through the chill ghostly air.

Whose shadow is that on the haunted ground?
Who's hiding behind that tree?
Oh, down the tree runs my bad black kitten,
And the shadow is only me!

Frances Frost

The Witches' Ride

Over the hills
Where the edge of the light
Deepens and darkens
To ebony night,
Narrow hats high
Above yellow bead eyes,
The tatter-haired witches
Ride through the skies.
Over the seas
Where the flat fishes sleep
Wrapped in the slap of the slippery deep,
Over the peaks
Where the black trees are bare,
Where bony birds quiver
They glide through the air.
Silently humming
A horrible tune,
They sweep through the stillness
To sit on the moon.

Karla Kuskin

Monster

No one will know me on Halloween,
I'll dress like a monster and act really mean,
I won't be quiet or gentle or sweet—
I'll be noisy and nasty when *I* trick or treat.
Then I'll hide all my loot on my closet shelf
And turn right back into—my wonderful self!

Judy Herbstman

On Halloween

On Halloween I'll go to town
And wear my trousers upside down,
And wear my shoes turned inside out
And wear a wig of sauerkraut.

Shel Silverstein

Skeleton Parade

The skeletons are out tonight,
They march about the street
With bony bodies, bony heads
And bony hands and feet.

Bony bony bony bones
With nothing in between
Up and down and all around
They march on Halloween.

Jack Prelutsky

Black and Gold

Everything is black and gold,
Black and gold tonight:
Yellow pumpkins, yellow moon,
Yellow candlelight;

Jet-black cat with golden eyes,
Shadows black as ink,
Firelight blinking in the dark
With a yellow blink.

Black and gold, black and gold,
Nothing in between—
When the world turns black and gold,
Then it's Halloween!

Nancy Byrd Turner

Nighttime Noises

Goblins chatter,
Footsteps clatter,
The night is crisp and clear.

Witches bustle,
Costumes rustle,
Halloween is here.

Deborah Zwecher

Acknowledgments

Grateful acknowledgment is made to the following for permission to reprint previously published material:

William Coles: "On Halloween" by Shel Silverstein. Copyright © 1961 by Shel Silverstein. Reprinted by permission of William Coles.

Aileen Fisher: "Fall" from THE COFFEE-POT FACE by Aileen Fisher, McBride, New York, 1933. Copyright renewed 1960. Reprinted by permission of the author.

Harcourt Brace Jovanovich, Inc.: "Hallowe'en" from THE LITTLE HILL, copyright 1949 by Harry Behn; copyright © 1977 by Alice L. Behn. Reprinted by permission of Harcourt Brace Jovanovich, Inc.

Harper & Row, Publishers, Inc.: Text of "The Witches' Ride" from THE ROSE ON MY CAKE by Karla Kuskin. Copyright © 1964 by Karla Kuskin. By permission of Harper & Row, Publishers, Inc.

Instructor: "Creepy" by Keith Hall, Jr., and "On Halloween" by Nina Willis Walter, *Instructor*, October 1971 and October 1972. Copyright © 1971, 1972 by The Instructor Publications, Inc. Used by permission.

McGraw-Hill Book Company: "Hallowe'en" from THE LITTLE WHISTLER by Frances Frost. Copyright 1949 by McGraw-Hill Book Company, Inc. Reprinted by permission of McGraw-Hill Book Company.

William Morrow & Company, Inc.: "Pumpkin" and "Skeleton Parade" from IT'S HALLOWEEN by Jack Prelutsky. Text copyright © 1977 by Jack Prelutsky. By permission of Greenwillow Books (A Division of William Morrow & Company).

Nancy Byrd Turner: "Black and Gold" by Nancy Byrd Turner. Copyright © 1956 by Nancy Byrd Turner. Reprinted by the kind permission of the Reverend Melvin Lee Steadman, Jr.